GIN

An Illustrated History

Tina Brown

AMBERLEY

To lovers of gin and history

Cover image courtesy of Zufanek.

First published 2018

Amberley Publishing
The Hill, Stroud
Gloucestershire, GL5 4EP

www.amberley-books.com

British Library Cataloguing in Publication Data.
A catalogue record for this book is available from the British Library.

ISBN 978 1 4456 8005 7 (print)
ISBN 978 1 4456 8006 4 (ebook)

Origination by Amberley Publishing.
Printed in Great Britain.

Contents

Introduction

Throughout history there doesn't seem to have been another drink that has quite rivalled the reputation of gin. Love it or loathe it, everyone seems to have an opinion on it. Since embarking on the research for this book I have gone on an incredible journey from ancient times right through to modern day and everything in between to try and find those snippets of gin's history that are not that well known about, the art and the architecture inspired by the drink, the people and the places connected to it and the impact gin has had on England and the world.

I have learnt about the design and creation of the bottles, which is something probably not thought about that much as many are more concerned about the contents of the bottle than what is on the outside. I have discovered the devastating effect that gin has had on so many of the population throughout history, in so many ways, and I have been amazed and inspired by the dedication of the modern gin creators and businesses of today.

When I first started my research for this book, I wasn't sure how the subject and idea would be received. I need not have worried; the gin world has been very friendly, open and supportive throughout my months of research, sending emails and nagging at businesses for copy and images, and throughout all that they have been so encouraging. I have written several books and am currently working on a few more, but I can honestly say that I have never had such a positive experience with contributors and people who have assisted me as I have done with this title and I would really like to thank them all for their kindness and generosity. I have also been forced to sample a few different gins and this has opened up a whole new experience for me – one of positive, aromatic delight, which I will share with you later in the book.

So how did gin begin? What is it made of and what started the current craze? To learn the answers to these and many more questions join me on this sensual exploration as we step back in time and discover some secrets about gin.

Illustration of a drunk leaving a gin shop from 1853. (Courtesy of the British Museum)

Chapter 1

So How Did it all Begin?

It's said gin has many medicinal qualities, including treating the plague!

Every age in history has enjoyed a tipple along the way; whether it be wine, beer, gin or some other beverage, each has played its own part in the society and history of the time. Alcoholic beverages are one aspect of society that has remained constant, and it is intriguing to think that the drinks we love and enjoy today were also consumed throughout history, and helped to shape not just our culture, but our societies.

So let's go back to Neolithic times, where there is archaeological evidence available to back up the understanding that people *c.* 10,000 BC were creating beverages by using the fermentation process. Archaeological testing on jars found in northern China from this time have revealed traces of alcohol that were absorbed into the ceramics and preserved. Traces of berries, hawthorn, grapes and rice were also found during the analysis, confirming that there was alcoholic drink-making activity during this period.

Chapter 2

Thirteenth Century:
The Plague and Gin

If there was one defining incident in the 1300s that had devastating consequences for the population of England it was when the bubonic plague swept through the country in 1348/49. It was estimated that some 20 per cent of the population of England lost their lives to the Black Death and some 25 million in total across Asia and Europe. Although at its most prominent in the 1300s, the plague intermittently returned in mass outbreaks up until the seventeenth century. From the very, very poor to the incredibly wealthy, the plague spared no one, although those who fell victim more quickly to the deadly clutches of the disease were the elderly, the sick and infants.

It was during these many outbreaks that the population would try anything in the hope that they could find some magical cure for the disease; the horrific swellings all over the body, the fevers and the sickness – people would have done anything to ease the suffering of so many. Some believed that bloodletting was a cure, others felt that drinking urine would benefit the victim and still others turned to gin for some relief. It is thought that the gin was topically applied and also consumed in an attempt to gain some respite from the desperate hand they had been dealt.

Chapter 3

Sixteenth and Seventeenth Century: The Start of Something New

Madam Genever was once sold from wheelbarrows in London's East End.

If, like myself, you have often wondered where the term 'Dutch courage' comes from, then read on. It is believed that English soldiers who were fighting in Antwerp against the Spanish in 1585, during the Eighty Years War, were partaking in genever as it had calming properties and helped many before embarking on war, giving them the courage to go forth and fight.

During the sixteenth and seventeenth centuries new laws changed the shape of the British countryside, with many fields being broken up with the use of blackthorn bushes, which resulted in the huge increase of sloes, which became abundant everywhere. With gin becoming popular during this period, it made sense to combine the two together and it was a way of turning the sometimes inedible sloes into something far more palatable.

The process of making sloe gin itself is one of history and tradition and making it gives you a sense of stepping back through the pages of an old recipe book from another age. The hardest part of the process is the long wait after you have made your creation before it becomes fit for consumption – sometimes up to three months.

Sloe gin is a red liqueur made with gin and sloe (blackthorn) drupes, which are a small fruit related to the plum. Tradition says that you soak them in gin and add sugar to ensure that the sloe juice is extracted from the fruit. Sloe gin is commercially created today by adding flavour to less expensive neutral grain spirits, although some makers do still use the more traditional methods.

Ancient makers wrote that the best sloes are picked after the first frost of winter (late October to early November). It was also interesting to note that when you prick the fruit this should be done with a thorn from the bush from which the sloes are to be picked from. Another bit of folklore was that you should never use a metal fork to prick the fruits unless it is silver.

For a traditional sloe gin you will need enough to half fill the bottle you are using, combined with 50g of sugar per litre of fluid.

Ingredients

- 500g ripe sloes
- 50g sugar
- 1 litre gin

Method

Ensure that you wash the sloes thoroughly and pick off any stems. Pat them dry with a clean tea towel or paper towel. Prick the sloes, or alternatively you can freeze them overnight and this will result in the skin splitting. Then you add the sloes to your clean

Nolet Distillery, the Netherlands, opened in 1691.

and sterilised bottle until it is half full. Add the gin and the sugar, seal it and leave for the required amount of time, ideally three months. Shake the bottle now and again to make sure that the sugar dissolves. When the magical time has finally arrived, strain the gin from the sloes by using a sieve of muslin cloth and re-seal the bottle and leave to enjoy.

Today there are annual sloe gin competitions and awards held up and down the country to find and honour the very best of the ancient sloe gin making in England.

It was in 1691 in Schiedam in the Netherlands that Joannes Nolet created the Nolet Distillery, which has an international reputation and is still producing gin today. Nolets has been handed down through the generations of the same family and has a remarkable history to tell. Joannes started his business at an interesting time in history with the medieval period coming to an end and new advancements being recognised in philosophy, politics, science and society. Jacobus Notlet (1682–1743) carried on what his father had set up and expended the distillery. He purchased a local windmill to ensure that there was always a supply of quality malt available to use in the production.

One of the earlier confirmations of the existence of gin dates from 1623, when it is mentioned in Philip Massinger's play *The Duke of Milan.*

Chapter 4

The Eighteenth Century: A Time of Smuggling and Other Illicit Happenings

The nickname of Mother's Ruin relates to the social problems caused by gin.

From the late 1690s, and pouring over into the first few decades of the 1700s, Dutch genever made its appearance in Britain with many cheap variants being brewed in the grimy and dirty dark alleyways of the capital city, which had devastating effects on London's poor. It was being sold for one penny for a dram or on a gin-soaked rag, making beggars out of its victims and resulting in crime and prostitution. It also contributed to a rise in infant mortality during this period.

By the 1730s, over 6,000 houses in London were openly selling gin to the general public. The drink was available in street markets, grocers, chandlers, barbers and brothels. Of 2,000 houses in one notorious district, more than 600 were involved in the retail of gin or in its production. A dram of gin cost a few pennies and a portion of the population became addicted to gin, but on the positive side, paid for their share of the war effort. On the negative, it destroyed the health of the people and created misery in its wake, with high crime and prostitution rates. Children drank too; perhaps it eased the terrible neglect in their lives as their parents lay drunk or driven mad by the spirit.

By 1736 gin consumption had reached new heights in England – or should I say new lows. Sellers of the drink even displayed signs outside their premises that stated: 'Drunk for one penny, dead drunk for two pence.'

Some premises kept their cellars full of straw in case their customers who were partaking in gin needed to sleep off its effects. The problem of the population drinking gin to excess was being recognised by doctors of the time, who said that gin was a cause of growing evils. One popular gin at this time was known as 'Old Tom', which was very different to the gins we consume today. It was a disgusting mix of copious amounts of sugar, to try and sweeten the foul base taste, and turpentine and sulphuric acid, which were also added to try and make the drink taste better – to little effect.

Something drastic had to be done and in 1736 Parliament imposed the Gin Act, which resulted in sellers of gin having to pay 20*s* per gallon sold and also required them

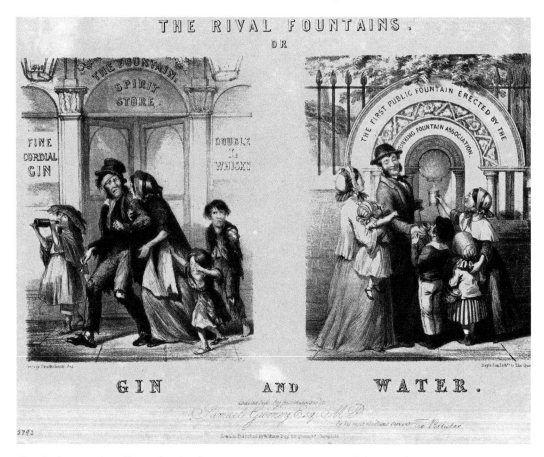

Sketch showing the effects of gin and water on society. (Courtesy of the British Museum)

to purchase a licence, which cost £50. This would have caused many sellers to cease trading and in one year the consumption of gin fell dramatically from 5.39 million to 3.6 million gallons.

However, this change did not last for long; riots started and then the illicit selling of gin began, which by 1743 saw things become far worse than they had been before. Therefore, in 1743 the fees for selling were reduced again and the licence fee was cut to £1. The situation did not improve though as in 1749 more than 4,000 sellers were convicted of selling without a licence and by the start of 1751 it was almost free trade, resulting in a significant rise in robbery, murder and disease throughout the population, which saw the civilised society deteriorating.

Later, in 1751, a new legislation was introduced that was moderate in action but which had successful results. The law stated that distillers could no longer sell to anyone who did not have a licence. Licences by this stage were very easy to obtain and unlicensed selling was not punished any more severely than before. The situation in 1758 was that duty was 1s per gallon and consumption had dropped to 2 million gallons per year, and these figures remained steady until 1780. However, following the rise of the price of gin, the poor turned elsewhere to find their comfort and way of escaping the horrors of life in the 1750s.

The words of historian and writer Henry Fielding at the time was that gin was 'the principal sustenance of more than 100,000 people'.

I come from a seaside town – Hastings in East Sussex, which is famous for the battle in 1066, its fishing heritage and maritime connections – and I have always immersed myself in the local history, which has fascinated me all my life. Along this stretch of the coast smuggling has always been prominent, with France being only 23 miles across the English Channel, offering the ideal opportunity for this illicit trade. Hastings has many connections with the smuggling history and in particular there are many stories and histories connected to the smuggling of gin, lace and tea into the country and wool and home manufactured goods out of the country.

There are stories of smuggling back in the fourteenth century when they were known as Owlers due to the signals they gave was the hoot of an owl.

There is a cottage set on a high pavement along the high street in the old quarter of Hastings, which has many smuggling stories attached to it. It is not surprising, therefore, that it is called Smugglers Cottage. It is a tiny red-bricked property with deep cellars that used to be connected to its neighbours. The cellars of this house were used by smugglers

Smugglers Cottage, Hastings, holds many secrets of the town's smuggling heritage. (Image courtesy of J. D. Neale)

Left and below: The Stag Inn, Hastings Old Town, is known for its connections with the smugglers, with deep cellars and secret tunnels. (Image courtesy of J. D. Neale)

INTERIOR VIEW of OLD PORTION of St. CLEMENTS CAVES, HASTINGS.

Old postcard of the caves at Hastings, which were once used to store smuggled gin.

carrying their goods; they could go into one house, down into the cellars and along a few houses, and this would hopefully confuse any customs guards who were following them. It is said that this house has the largest chimney in the whole of the town and it was used for hiding contraband goods.

Another building closely linked with the smugglers is The Stag Inn in All Saints Street. This is an ancient public house, with the site once being an old ale house in the fourteenth century and the present building being constructed in the sixteenth century. Again this is a property with deep cellars that used to connect to the East Hill cliffs behind the property, the churchyard of All Saints at the top of the street and to many other houses in the street. In the past bottles and caskets of gin have been found along the tunnels and passageways once used by the smugglers who would have brought the boats ashore and carried their goods up through the tunnels to the Stag Inn, together with barrels of beer and gold coins.

In another part of East Sussex you will find the village of Friston, nestled on the South Downs. Much of the area around Friston is arable and has been for centuries, with much of the local population being involved in agricultural work at one stage or another. If you explore this village you will find a house called Crowlink and it is here in its deep cellars in the 1800s that gin was discovered, described as full to bursting. The goods would have been landed close by at a nearby cove on the coastline.

I am sure that this story of smuggling along the coasts of Britain is far from unique, but it does go some way to show how much a part of history gin is and how it has helped shape the society we now know today.

It is not surprising that there is more about the history of gin during the 1700s and 1800s than other periods, and it was in 1751 that English artist William Hogarth brought to life in his images the horrors of drinking the alcoholic beverage and the effects on society it was having. The print *Gin Lane*, together with another called *Beer Street*, was issued in support of what would become the Gin Act and depicted the contrast between drinking beer and consuming gin. Around this time a friend of Hogarth's, Henry Fielding, published *An Inquiry into the Late Increase in Robbers*, together with *The Four Stages of Cruelty*, exploring the problems of poverty and crime and their connection with gin.

In *Beer Street* the inhabitants appear to be happy and healthy and nutritionally fulfilled on their diet of English ale. However, in stark contrast, those in *Gin Lane* display the attributes of an addict; starvation, madness, decay, suicide and death. *Gin Lane* was set in the notorious slum areas of London and portrays the negativity and desperation of a community consumed by gin. One character that many remember is that of the women in the foreground of the picture who appears aged by gin and forced into prostitution by her addiction and habit. She has sores on her legs, which are a symptom of syphilis, and

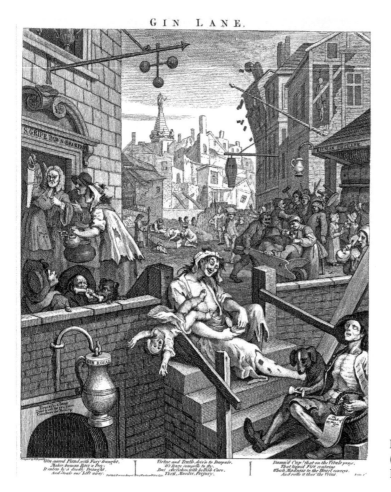

Hogarth's *Gin Lane*.
(Courtesy of the British Museum)

her baby is shown falling into the gin cellar to its death below. Her clothes are draped across her and she appears to have no regard for her half naked appearance, with her only concern being gin.

Many felt that Hogarth's images were a huge exaggeration of the subject and were illustrated in such a way to encourage the Gin Act being enforced. However, the depiction of the woman was a sight sadly too common on the streets of London, with stories being told of small babies and children being reclaimed by their mothers from the workhouse after having been given a new set of clothes, only to be strangled and left in a ditch so that the clothes could be sold to pay for more gin. There are other stories of a woman who let a young child burn to death while she slept on in a gin-induced stupor.

Meanwhile, the Dutch gin production had reached new heights and Joannes Nolet II (1712–1772) of the famous Nolet family exported his father's genever for the first time. The town of Schiedam became the centre of Holland's distilling industry and Nolet became a distinguished member of the Distillers Guild. Nolets also supported local charities in their work. The family has a long tradition of Dutch distillery business, which is still in operation today. Joannes Nolet III (1747–1835) became mayor of the town and saw the construction of several windmills in the area, which was partly financed by the Nolets. It was during this period that further, significant expansions were seen at the Nolet Distillery. It was to be the next generation of the family, Jacobus Nolet (1773–1811), who would take the transatlantic journey and became good friends with John Adams, who was later to become President of the United States. And so the international journey of gin had begun.

In the north of England you will find the town of Warrington, and it is here that Thomas Dakin is recognised as the creator of modern gin. In 1761 he founded his first

Ceramic bin label produced 1760–1860 by Wedgewood Pottery. (Image courtesy of York Museums Trust, http://yorkmuseumstrust.org.uk/, CC BY – SA 4.0)

A Van Hoboken ceramic, The Netherlands. Created to celebrate the company's 150th year in 1925.

distillery at the age of twenty-five in Bright Street, Warrington, and it was believed to be the first distillery outside of London. Dakin was a strong believer in offering a quality gin product, away from the old-style cheap gin that had taken over the country so far. His distillery and his products were hugely popular in the local market, and with its nearby ports in Liverpool this meant that sailors, travellers and people who worked on the water were among the first people to sample Dakin's gin. Today, the inspiration for the bottles is still taken from the original glass designs from the 1800s, which started the business and still flourishes today.

It was in 1769 that Alexander Gordon, the founder of Gordon's London dry gin, opened his first distillery. His idea was to provide a quality drink after so much poor quality gin had been produced for so long. In 1786 he moved his factory to take advantage of purer water from the natural spring at Clerk's Well (Clerkenwell).

It was during the 1700s that another amazing, lifesaving discovery was made, in the form of quinine, by a Scottish doctor by the name of George Gleghorn, who discovered that not only could it be used to prevent the disease, but also to cure it.

Gutter Children, a sketch showing the effects of gin on society. (Courtesy of the British Museum)

Chapter 5

Nineteenth Century: Gin Palaces and So Much More

G&T, the most famous cocktail of all time.

A fascinating insight into gin drinking culture from the early 1800s can be seen in a recent archaeological discovery in Poland, close to Gdańsk, in the form of stoneware gin bottles on a shipwreck, pointing towards the evidence that sailors of this time enjoyed the odd tipple of gin. Those involved in the complex research have suggested that the vessels could contain a type of gin with an alcohol content of 14 per cent. This was discovered alongside intact, and fragmented, ceramic and metal vessels, including a tall, stoneware bottle, which had been perfectly preserved and corked, and embossed with the writing 'Selter', suggesting that its contents might be soda water produced for several centuries close to the village of the same name in the Taunus mountain range in Germany. The archaeologist connected with the project and the National Maritime Museum reported that it was felt that the discovery contained 14 per cent alcohol, which had been diluted, possibly with that of Selter soda water. It was later added that from the laboratory analysis of the contents of the bottle that it may be a type of genever (or jenever) gin.

Pre-1818 there was no way to test the strength of a spirit and so the Navy started adding grains to their gunpowder to tests its alcoholic strength. If it failed to light then it was diluted gin. They discovered that only gin that was 114 per cent proof (or 57 per cent in today's measures) could light the gunpowder – weaker measures didn't.

It was in the 1840s that the British in the tropical colonies started to use gin to mask the bitter flavour of quinine, which was the only effective anti-malarial product available at the time. Quinine had to be dissolved in fizzy water to form a tonic water and therefore the result when it was added to gin was 'gin and tonic'. Modern tonics on the market today only contain a trace of quinine, used as a flavouring.

In the mid-1800s the pink gin, or Pink Plymouth, took drinkers by storm and appeared on cocktail menus far and wide. In 1887 this mix was called 'fiz' and later was hugely popular in America. In some bars special bartenders were hired just to create fiz for their clientele. The cocktail consisted of Plymouth Gin and a dash of Angostura Bitters (a dark red bitter that gave the drink the pink colour it was famous for). Lemon rind was added as a garnish, giving a hint of citrus taste and aroma to compliment the beverage.

Another change that came about during this period was the idea, setup and functionality of the pub. Prior to this time the pub had been in a terraced house; there was nothing special about the location, and it was set in a ground floor front room, which was a public area. Pubs were a common meeting place for people who knew each other to meet and have a drink in comfort; however, as times changed, so did the pub, and a counter was installed so that only the pub workers could have access to the alcohol. From the 1830s the homely informal pub was becoming more formal and run more like a business. The 'bar' became the centrepiece of the pub, with an area behind the bar that was out of bounds unless the landlord invited you as this was a private sitting room and not open to the public. Jug and bottle departments were later set up, where customers could bring their own jugs to collect alcohol for home consumption.

There were also several rooms in the pub. These consisted of the taprooms, which were the cheap rooms, with wooden tables and benches, while the bar parlour retained more of its domestic style furnishings. Different rooms catered for different customers and it was hoped that certain pubs would attract regular customers. In *Sketches by Boz*, Dickens describes two London pubs as attracting 'steady old boys' and that they are 'always in the same taverns at the same hours every evening'. Here they would sit together and tell stories and smoke and drink, or on occasion they were a meeting point, from where people would go to the theatre and later return. Other pubs were more of a function, in that people who were using the coaches could meet there or people meeting travellers from the coaches could partake in a drink – this is seen today at the railway stations. And so it was that pubs were to become a regular part of life on all main thoroughfares where the public walked past, each pub hoping that it would attract more new customers. Even in new areas of construction, pubs were being built; gone were the times of the 'sitting in someone's front room' feel, pubs were now being specifically designed and built for areas. Often in new areas of construction pubs were the first building to be created, and thus they were popular with the workers.

However, in the 1830s the pub was facing a new competitor for its customers – the gin palace. Many of the less popular pubs were being turned into these more elaborate and decorative drinking establishments. The buildings were described as:

> Once ... a low dirty public house with only one doorway, [it has] been transformed into a splendid edifice, the front ornamented with pilasters, supporting a handsome cornice and entablature and the whole elevation being remarkably striking and handsome; the doorways were increased in number from one small one to three and each of them being eight to ten feet wide. The doors and the windows were glazed with very large single squares of plate glass and the gas fittings of the most costly description. Until midnight, when the doors were opened the rush was tremendous, it was instantly filled with customers.

Gas lighting and the plate glass windows made the new gin palace a place of luxury for many and places of warmth and light for others who had very little of either.

Dark brown serving bottle dated 1820–60. (Image courtesy of York Museums Trust, http://yorkmuseumstrust.org.uk/, CC BY – SA 4.0)

Everyday Life, Everyday People, from *Sketches by Boz,* 1836. (Courtesy of the British Museum)

Charles Dickens noted that the poorer an area, the grander the gin palace is. He also wrote that in 1835, amid the filth and despair of St Giles in London, that the places were:

> Light and brilliancy ... the gay building with the fantastically ornamented parapet, the illuminated clock, the plate glass windows surrounded by stucco rosettes and its gas lights with richly gilt burners, they are perfectly dazzling when contrasted with the darkness and dirt we have just left.

The internal decoration of a gin palace was often described as being more elaborate and gayer then the outside of the buildings, with displays of French polished mahogany and carved wood, and being equally well furnished throughout. Some customers of the time are described as being in stark contrast to the ornateness and stylish surroundings they are drinking in – two washerwomen, two old men who had finished their third quarters of gin (quarter of a pint) and are crying drunk, and some elderly women drinking rum shrub (mixture of rum, lemon and sugar). There were reported to have been a constant stream of customers in all shapes, sizes and ages into the gin palaces – men, women and children, poor, sick and wealthy all frequented these new places.

Gin barrel from 1800–37, used in hotels and retail during this period. Stoneware keg with metal tap and Royal Coat of Arms. (Image courtesy of York Museums Trust, http://yorkmuseumstrust.org.uk/, CC BY – SA 4.0)

Stephen Geary, born 31 August 1797, was one of the great Victorian entrepreneurs. Among his successes was the design for The Bell Inn in Pentonville Road, London, which was the first public house in the city. Later he was to design and open the first gin palace the country had seen in Aldgate, London. Geary's creation was described as having many handsome features, including plate glass, brilliant gaslight and luxuriously lavish mahogany counters, designed with glittering mirrors on all walls. This all helped to create a lively atmosphere where people could have a good time, and which was seen as a gathering place for the public.

By the 1840s the palaces were exuding glamour, but one principal feature that they were lacking in was seating. The idea of the palace at that time was that there was comfort for the customer to purchase the drink, consume it quickly, leave and then return later for another drink and to spend more. In the 1850s the palaces were divided with separate bars providing different drinking experiences for their different clientele – the jug and bottle entrance, the wholesale bar and the retail bar.

You can gain an understanding from Dickens and other writers at the time of how much of a positive experience it must have been for many of the population to visit these new places when you considered what their everyday lives and living condition were

A figurine from 1826–42 produced by Rockingham Works and Brameld & Co. (Potterys) depicting the effects of gin and water. (Image courtesy of York Museums Trust, http://yorkmuseumstrust.org.uk/, CC BY – SA 4.0)

like, let alone the disease and crime many were subjected to. I can see how the gin palace was addictive and how these palaces may have also helped fuel a downward spiral for many lonely souls in society. It was felt that the design of the gin palaces was related to that of department stores found in London or Paris.

Some Victorians, however, had another use for gin, with reports of some women using it to wash clothes in. One London workhouse documented in 1856 that the doctors' assistants were given slightly better food than the patients they were meant to be looking after and that they were given more gin, with many reports of them being drunk by 7 a.m. Moreover, if there was a corpse that needed laying out then they would receive an extra glass of gin for doing this task.

There was seldom much – if any – enjoyment in Victorian London for the poor, and even the positive experiences were often tinged with something dark. Dog fighting and other animal and cock fighting went on in pits throughout the poorer parts of the city, often late into the night, but this was not everyone's cup of tea. Other people frequented the theatres and music halls, of which there was a variety to suit all tastes. Children from the slums often visited the 'Penny Gaffs', a kind of local neighbourhood theatre that squeezed up to six performances into an evening to an audience of around 200 people. The audience was aged between eight and twenty and was mainly made up of women. The acts, however, were described as being crude, foul and filthy, being made up on rude songs and filthy dancing by the male and female artists. The Penny Gaff was described as the place where juvenile crime meets juvenile poverty and were the dingiest, dirtiest of places, with the odour being almost unbearable to stand. However, the audience and actors' thirst for gin was high, some drinking a glass, others a half pint and some a pint. It is no surprise that many fights and reports of crimes were common, with gin being blamed for fuelling such activity.

On a more positive note there were many who saw the gin palaces as good for the soul and the people, as an article from the *Dundee Courier* dated 28 December 1871 describes:

> The Gin Palaces were decked with Christmas decorations. Miss this and Mr that, great floral artists of the time have been engaged to decorate the Magpie and Stump of the Goose in the highest style of art and with floral profusion never yet witnessed in any establishment of the kind. This will show great enterprise and will give Christmas character and cheer to the street. The public house is really a banquet hall, club room and smoking den all in one for middle and poorer classes and the décor is considerate as well as reasonable.

Somewhere that has nineteenth-century gin connections in Hastings is an area situated in the town centre known as the America Ground. This area has its roots back in the twelfth century when Hastings was first created. At that time much depended on the harbour; however, many storms during the thirteenth century totally destroyed the harbour area, resulting in the downturn of the fishing village Hastings had become known as. It took centuries of work to try and replace this harbour, with eventually the marshy land becoming solid ground, which in the nineteenth century saw developments starting to take shape. By 1815 substantial trade existed and flourished under the guidance of some of Hasting's most influential families at that time. Business such as bakers, millers and pig keepers functioned and traded in this area, which had once been deprived and forgotten. However, many from outside of the area said that the America Ground was still a poor area, consumed by crime and disease. What truth there is in this we do not know, but one thing we do recognise is the establishment of a school in the area that is said to have been the forerunner of the William Parker School, which still continues today, so it cannot have been all that bad. Another business that had huge success was the Black Horse gin palace. Perhaps they were supplied by the contraband frequently brought ashore in this area.

It was during the late 1850s that the rise of the gin and tonic took place. Its life began in India following a large number of British citizens migrating there with their families to serve the Crown, taking gin, their favourite drink, with them. However, many of the immigrants soon became infected with malaria, resulting in huge health concerns, especially regarding the soldiers. They were advised to take quinine, which is an anti-malarial alkaloid that is extracted from the bark of the cinchona tree. However, due to its bitter, unpleasant taste many of them refused. So a solution was found, and that was in the form of adding gin to quinine, which resulted in a much more palatable drink, with medicinal benefits. And so the gin and tonic, the world's most simple cocktail, was born. Next time you have a gin and tonic, spare a thought for its humble beginnings.

The next step in the history of the Nolet Distillery in the Netherlands was to be taken by Joannes Nolet (1801–1861), who again took the family business to new levels – so much so that in the mid-1800s the distillery moved to a new location at Hoofdstraat, which is still its current premises. The move was greatly helped by the access to the distribution networks through shipping, railways and canals that were springing up all over Europe.

It was Jacobus Nolet (1836–1906) who made advancements with the hand-stoked coal-fired alembic copper pot stills, which are still used today and from which their brand gets its name, Ketel One. By this time the produce was being shipped internationally.

During 1867 Parliament made is compulsory to add lime or lemon to antiscorbutics (treatment for scurvy) in an attempt to help with this condition and so that sailors on board ships had access to medical treatments. The Royal Navy's doctor, Sir Thomas Desmond Gimlette, added Navy Strength gin to 'fortify' and lime cordial to 'immunise'. This later became known as the Gimlet.

The following old gin bottles, discovered in New Zealand and dating from the mid-1800s, were discovered during archaeological excavations.

The Van Dulken Weiland bottle, which would have contained genever, is from around the 1850s to 1870s and was found in an old gully in central Christchurch, NZ, which was gradually filled in during the 1860s and 1870s.

The Sir Robert Burnett Old Tom gin bottle was found in a large rubbish pit on the site of a nineteenth-century bonded warehouse on Oxford Terrace, in the central city. Two warehouses were built on the site, one in 1864 and one in 1873–74: the gin bottle is likely associated with the second of these. Large quantities of broken bottles were found in this and other rubbish pits on the site, many of them still labelled and/or sealed, suggesting that they had been stock that broke or went off and had to be discarded.

The Bols gin bottle and Blankenheim and Nolet bottles were both found on the site of the Occidental Hotel, previously known as the Collins Family Hotel, which was first established in Christchurch's central city in 1861. The bottles were likely used in the 1870s to 1880s.

Van Dulken Weiland gin. (Image courtesy of J. Garland, Underground Overground Archaeology)

Bols gin bottle. (Image courtesy
of M. L. Bernabeu, Underground
Overground Archaeology)

0 cm   5 cm

0 cm   5 cm

Blankenheim & Nolet stoneware gin bottle.
(Image courtesy of M. L. Bernabeu, Underground
Overground Archaeology)

Old Tom gin bottle.
(Image courtesy of
J. Garland, Underground
Overground Archaeology)

0 cm   5 cm

Small Rotterdam
bottle,
nineteenth century.

Rotterdam
bottles,
nineteenth
century.

Chapter 6

Twentieth Century: Bathtub Gin, the War Year and More

The Junipers grow on an evergreen bush.

It was Joannes Nolet (1867–1934) who opened a distillery in Baltimore, USA, after falling in love with the country. However, despite the drink's huge successes throughout the country, it was hampered by Prohibition, with Joannes giving up its production there.

'A Drop of the Hollands' postcard from the early 1900s.

Many of us forget that the rubbish we throw away today will one day be someone's discovery, bringing to life the past of our period, and this is just what happened in a town in Israel called Ramla, where British soldiers were camped during the First World War. A remarkable discovery of hundreds of gin and whisky bottled was unearthed by archaeologists working on the site. The bottles were found among broken pieces of pottery and cutlery in a rubbish tip, which give a unique and colourful insight into the lives of the British soldiers when they were based there. The reports suggest that the majority of the discarded items in the pit were those of liquor bottles, showing that the soldiers would have taken advantage of the alcohol available to them to help relieve the worry and stresses of the situations they were faced with. The information gleaned from this find will be able to offer archaeologists a unique opportunity to be able to step back in time and help them piece together what everyday life was like for the soldiers and for the military as a whole at this point in our history.

The First World War also saw a sharp increase in women drinking alcohol. With the continuous worries of money, losing loved ones and the plight of the country, many turned to alcohol, namely gin, for its soothing qualities and comfort.

The wonderfully named Bathtub Gin refers to a gin that is made at home in amateur conditions and not those of a professional distillery. The earliest reference of this name was in 1920s in the United States, and it was then also used to describe a drink of poor quality. Many of the bottle used at the time were too large to fit under standard taps and so the taps on the bathtub were used to add water, providing the name. Many of

Comic cartoon postcard.

Magazine advert from 1951 for Holloway London Gin.

the cocktails created were done to hide the unpleasant taste the Bathtub Gin had, and therefore they owe their existence to the home brew. Today, Bathtub Gin is also the name for a gin brand produced by Ableforth's in the United Kingdom.

The 1920s really were the time for gin and saw its popularity rise once more. People were experimenting more by mixing and adding different flavours. Throughout the Roaring Twenties and into the early 1930s gin was glamorised by the glitz of the fashion of the time and more and more women were drinking large amounts of alcohol, gin included, than ever before.

During the Second World War desperate measures were implemented in the form of food rationing, which was felt harder by those living in the towns and cities than those with a rural existence, who were able to some extent support themselves by growing their own produce. However, despite rationing restrictions some items could always be obtained on the black market or if you had the correct commodities to deal in. The economy itself at this time had little in the way of cash and so a whole host of items would be used in the bartering and exchange of desired goods.

The humble egg proved to be one of the most popular and desirable items to trade off for items that were considered more of a luxury; for example, for products such as cigarettes, dried fruits and gin! Many hoteliers during this period were known to go to great lengths to impress their clientele with the food they could offer and there were reports of them travelling from the towns and cities with bottles of gin in hand to farms where they would trade this for produce.

The Nolet unique history continued and it was during the time when the threat of the Second World War loomed largely over Europe. Paulus Nolet (1915–2001) recognised how the threats of war could severely damage the Schiedam Distillery. The occupying troops seized stocks and production was significantly reduced due to lack of labour and raw materials.

Carolus Nolet (b. 1941) launched a new premium genever in 1979 called the Kotel 1, which was inspired by reading his ancestors' notes regarding small pot distilleries, and this has remained a strong brand in the gin market.

Today, the family business is continued by brothers Bob and Carl, who grew up playing in the distillery and playing football in the warehouses. The have been brought up surrounded by the sights, smells and sounds of the distillery, and it is a huge part of their lives.

Chapter 7

Present Day:
A Voyage of Gin Discovery

Old Tom refers to a large number of historical gins from the eighteenth and nineteenth centuries. Some distillers are trying to bring to life the past in modern-day versions.

During the writing of this book, I approached many businesses and individuals connected with gin in the hopes of gleaning a greater understanding of modern-day gins and the unique histories behind their brands. I will be forever grateful for the support each of the contributors have given me and the words of encouragement, and of course the samples of much-needed gin supplied throughout my research.

So if you are interested in the more unique brands of today and want to learn about their own histories and what has inspired them to create the gins of today, please read on. These are the gin history of today and for future generations to discover. Let me introduce you to the makers!

Silent Pool Distillers

Drawn by a common passion for craft distilling, a group of friends came together to create a new kind of distillery, producing handcrafted, artisan spirits with uncompromising quality. In an extraordinary location on the Duke of Northumberland's Albury Estate, a group of dilapidated farm buildings on the banks of the legendary Silent Pool has been transformed to become the home of the Silent Pool Distillers.

In keeping with the original vision for a sustainable business, a vintage wood-fired steam boiler was restored to power the hand-built copper still, created for Silent Pool Distillers by the Arnold Holstein Company in the Lake Constance area of Germany.

The distillery was completed with the arrival of the bespoke stainless steel tanking, sourced from the Vipara Valley in Slovenia – tanking designed to hold both the spirit and the crystal-clear water used to make delicious spirits.

Right and below: Silent Pool
Distilleries.

Silent Pool Distilleries.

Sacred Gin, London

It is estimated that back in eighteenth-century London, during the infamous 'Gin Craze', there were an astonishing 1,500 distilleries in the capital. Today there is only a handful, the smallest and most unusual being the award-winning Sacred micro-distillery, located in Ian Hart's family home in Highgate, North London. The first and smallest commercial distillery of its kind, and certainly the only one based in a residential house, it has quickly built up a loyal and enthusiastic following – Sacred Gin was awarded a double gold medal at the San Francisco World Spirits Competition.

For many years Ian had collected – and enjoyed drinking – old Bordeaux red wines, but he also appreciated a good gin and tonic. He had often thought about creating his own London dry gin and, as a Londoner, he also liked the idea of producing what is traditionally a London product actually in London. In September 2008 he decided to make a serious effort to realise this ambition.

Ian has always been interested in science – he has a degree in Natural Sciences – and decided to turn traditional gin production on its head by using vacuum distillation rather than a traditional pot still. Vacuum distillation occurs at a much lower temperature (35–45°C) than pot distillation (85–95°C) so the distillates are lusher and fresher – think of the marmalade flavour of cooked oranges versus fresh cut oranges. Ian enthusiastically set about experimenting with many different gin formulas, distilling dozens of well-known and obscure botanicals, and every Sunday evening he would take his latest gin recipe into his local pub, The Wrestlers, for people to try.

Sacred Gin Distillery.

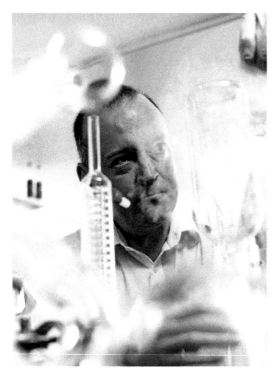

Left and below: Ian from Sacred Gin with glassware.

Sacred Gin preparing the ingredients for their gins.

Left: Sacred Christmas Pudding Gin bottle.

Below: Sacred Gin.

In early 2009 he was persuaded by this ad hoc panel of gin tasters that his twenty-third recipe, which has a fresh, creamy and aromatic quality, was the unique gin Ian had been looking for. It contains twelve botanicals including juniper, cardamom, nutmeg and *Boswellia sacra* (aka Hougary Frankincense), hence the name.

However, it is not just its production methods that make Sacred so special: Ian has accumulated a library of over 100 botanicals he has distilled purely out of interest – buddleia, oak bark and lemon verbena for example – and tasting and blending these inevitably led to the creation of new recipes such as Sacred Spiced English Vermouth, made from English wine and twenty-four botanicals, including organic wormwood from Somerset, macerated plum and cherry stones from Gloucestershire and cubeb from Indonesia. This quite naturally progressed to Sacred Rosehip Cup, the fruitier English alternative to Campari, so that it is now possible to enjoy an entirely Sacred Negroni!

Encouraged by the success of Sacred Gin, Ian has created Sacred Organic Gin, Sacred Organic Sloe Gin (with extra juniper) plus seven additional gins, each of which focuses on a particular key botanical – juniper, coriander, cardamom, pink grapefruit, orris, liquorice and Christmas pudding – plus Sacred Organic Vodka, Sacred London Dry Vodka, Sacred Amber Vermouth and Sacred Extra Dry Vermouth and Sacred Bottle-Aged Negroni.

Most recently Sacred English Peated Whisky and Sacred Whisky Liqueur were added to the range. Not surprisingly, Ian realised he was in urgent need of some additional space, so Sacred moved into new premises above the Star pub in Highgate – approximately 100 yards from Karl Marx's grave. This means that while Ian is still able to carry on distilling at home, he now has the capacity to significantly increase production and is also able to host distillery visits and gin tasting events. It is a very exciting time for Sacred, the spirit of innovation!

www.sacredgin.com

The Wrecking Coast Distiller, Tintagel, Cornwall

The Wrecking Coast Distillery based in Tintagel, Cornwall, and run by four friends, Avian Sandercock, Daniel Claughton, Steve Wharton and Craig Penn, proudly launch their premium Cornish Clotted Cream Gin – Born in Tintagel, Born to be Enjoyed!

Why Did We Start Our Particular Journey into the World of Distilling?

Craig Penn, one of the four founders at The Wrecking Coast Distillery, explains:

> Simple really, it was born out of a desire to drink a gin that suited our taste. We were looking for a smooth gin, a gin that was built from the ground up to hit the right balance of flavours. We didn't want to adjust a gin to make it smooth, we wanted to build a gin around the smoothness.

The Smoothness of Clotted Cream

Avian Sandercock, master distiller at The Wrecking Coast Distillery, feels the answer comes from local inspiration:

> We had an idea of our gin providing a luxurious feel, smooth on the palate but remaining true to the core flavours of gin. From the outset we thought the icon of Cornwall, clotted cream, would provide that luxurious feel, the smoothness and add a subtle hint of vanilla. As Craig said, our idea was to construct a gin around the clotted cream to enable the distinctly luxurious feel in our gin.
>
> It was essential that we captured the velvety richness of the clotted cream, but this caused us a few challenges. In the production of clotted cream, the cream is baked, giving the iconic golden crust and smooth, firm cream beneath. But when heated the cream will separate and the flavours become more caramel than cream.
>
> We found a solution by using a hand blown, glass vacuum still, built to our own specification, to distil the neutral spirit and fresh clotted cream mix. This results in a crystal clear spirit that retains the flavour of the cream, together with the velvety richness of the texture.

This is something all of the founders are particularly proud of. Craig highlights this unique approach:

> This constantly hands-on process means we can only make very small quantities at a time. However, it is this small detail in our unique gin that makes the big difference. It is what makes The Wrecking Coast Gin so distinctive.

Our Cutting-Edge Still

In selecting their still, The Wrecking Coast Distillery did a large amount of research. Traditional thinking leads most distillers to either a variation of the ancient alembic still or a modified European fruit still, but they wanted to bring their gin into the twenty-first century. Avian explains:

> We wanted to be able to put all our efforts into constructing a new gin around the clotted cream and not into coaxing old technology to life. We kept coming back to iStill, a Dutch company run by Odin, the genius behind their computer-controlled stills. We travelled out to Woerden in Holland, the birthplace of gin, to meet him and hit it off straight away. His technology matched exactly what we wanted to achieve and his depth of knowledge and passion for distilling was only matched by his boundless enthusiasm and genuine desire for us to produce the best gin we can.

The Wrecking Coast Clotted Cream Gin

To capture the essence of The Wrecking Coast and its Premium Cornish Clotted Cream Gin, local artist and Camelford Gallery owner John Blight was commissioned to provide a unique piece of art. This is the foundation of the gin's label that is applied, numbered and signed by hand.

www.thewreckingcoastdistillery.com

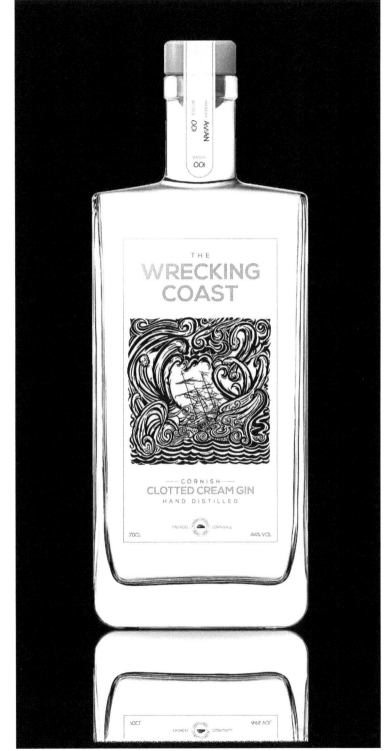

Wrecking Coast Gin.

Salcombe Gin

Born out of a love of gin, and a dream to produce the finest white spirit in the world within one of England's most stunning coastal towns, Salcombe Gin has been scooping awards for its exceptionally smooth taste since 2016. Like most good ideas, it all began with a conversation over a gin and tonic in a bar between co-founders Angus and Howard.

Hampshire-born Howard Davies got his first taste of nautical pursuits at the age of five, during long sailing weekends and summer holidays in Salcombe. With a deep yearning to live on the coast, it wasn't long before the family moved down to Salcombe, and Howard spent his childhood out on the water.

It was while teaching sailing as a teenager at the Island Cruising Club in Salcombe that Howard met Angus Lugsdin – a fellow young instructor at the club, who had learnt to sail in Salcombe and spent every family holiday messing around on boats. After strenuous days sailing the azure waters of South Devon, they would head to shore to kick-start the evening over gin and tonics on the terrace at Salcombe Yacht Club.

As life tugged them into the real world, they each went their separate ways. Howard's path took him to Oxford University to study engineering while representing the university in international sailing races as a Full Blue. He then carved out a career as a management consultant in the city. When the call of the ocean became too much, he left his job and travelled the world teaching sailing and windsurfing in Sydney, the Greek islands and the Maldives. After several years, winds of change brought Howard back to Devon, this time to set up a number of businesses of his own.

In the meantime, Angus studied marine geography at Cardiff University before embarking on a career offshore, mapping the world's oceans. This led to long stints based out in Asia and in the Gulf of Mexico working for clients including BP and Shell. From 2006 Angus lived in Manhattan working for a small public company with a focus on underwater security. It was here in the States that Angus witnessed the craft distilling movement, which cultivated his passion for single malt whisky. He followed his curiosities to the renowned Springbank Distillery in Scotland. One of the last surviving producers of Campbeltown Single Malts, this distillery produces handmade whisky in the most traditional way.

Inspired by the authentic process during his time spent distilling whisky, and unable to shake off the persistent nagging that he should go into the spirits business himself, Angus challenged himself to build a business plan by the end of the year. With this in mind, he called upon his old friend Howard for his business acumen and friendship, knowing that Howard too was looking for a change.

Together they recognised an increasing demand among consumers for spirits with genuine provenance, quality and character. After devising a clear business plan and gaining the support of key investors, they set about crafting their own exceptional spirit in small batches.

After eighteen months of whipping up daily batches, tweaking the recipe day by day, and endless tastings, they created the perfectly balanced gin that we love today. The zesty blend of grapefruit, lemon and lime is a nod to the famous Salcombe 'Fruiters', who imported over 80 per cent of the citrus fruit coming to England during the nineteenth century.

Off the coast at Salcombe.

Delicious Salcombe Gin.

Above and right: Creators of Salcombe Gin.

Salcombe still.

Creating Salcolme Gin.

Harbouring distinct notes of ruby red grapefruit, along with the heady, earthy pine notes of the finest Macedonian juniper, Salcombe Gin is the perfect balance of aromas and flavours with an amazing lingering finish.

Caspyn Gin, Cornwall

Pocketful of Stones was born in the cellar of a pub in London. Sat around a tiny copper still, two brothers tinkered with gin recipe after gin recipe. The dream was to get back to their roots, the outdoors and the ocean, and to produce something they were both passionate about. Thus, Caspyn was born.

> Everything we create at Pocketful of Stones Distillers, whether it be gin, liqueurs, absinthe or whisky, we do through our senses. Smell is huge, as is taste, but sight and feel have a big roll too. A gin needs to look good, smell good, taste and feel good, and by automating the process how are you going to be able to achieve all of that?
>
> Everything we do is by the centuries old techniques of distillation, no computers are programmed, nothing is automated, it's a lot more work but I wouldn't change it for the world. Caspyn are a small craft distillery close to Penzance, Cornwall. Caspyn strive to produce everything with the upmost integrity and respect of the ingredients and the environment which makes our recipes.

Supporters of the Cornish Wildlife Trust, every bottle of Caspyns sold helps with wildlife conservation in Cornwall.

The Caspyn Gin and Tonic

We like our gin and tonic the way it's been served for decades but you can tart it up if you'd like. Think rosemary, pink pepper corns, edible flowers... And of course, we like ours a double. You'll need:

- 50ml Caspyn Gin
- A dash of tonic – more if required
- Ice and a slice of lemon. Boom!

www.caspyn.com

Caspyn Gin.

Caspyn Gin Distillery.

Wicked Wolf Exmoor Gin – The Spirit of Exmoor®

Launched in September 2015, Wicked Wolf Exmoor Gin is a premium craft gin made from eleven botanicals, distilled and blended on the banks of the picturesque River Lyn, North Devon. Passionate about gin, husband and wife team Pat Patel and Julie Heap are the faces behind this exciting venture. Wicked Wolf Exmoor Gin uses the perfect combination of eleven exotic botanicals producing complex layers of citrus and pepper notes finely balanced with the distinct flavours of juniper and coriander, resulting in a mature, premium spirit. Hibiscus, cardamom and kaffir lime leaves have been artfully blended with these traditional aromatics, creating a full-flavoured, smooth gin. Pot distilled in a copper alembic still, Wicked Wolf Exmoor Gin is lovingly blended, filtered, bottled and labelled by hand in exclusive 100-litre batches. They currently produce a minimum of two batches a week, and plan to expand to seven batches per week by the end of the year.

Each aromatic is prepared by hand, and are infused and distilled separately, resulting in elven individual distillates that are then skilfully blended. This approach allows complete control over the strength of each flavour, and enables consistency across each batch.

Wicked Wolf Exmoor Gin.

Pat Patel and Julie Heap, Wicked Wolf founders.

Wicked Wolf Exmoor Gin.

The gin is filtered at each stage of the production process, producing a 42 per cent ABV, smooth, full-bodied and elegant spirit.

Wicked Wolf Gin is served with ice and lime over a sprig of thyme – this really does enhance all the flavours. It is equally at home neat with a block or two of ice, mixed with a quality tonic and garnished with pink grapefruit, in a classic gin martini or in a Negroni.

www.wickedwolfgin.com | www.facebook.com/wickedwolfgin | @wickedwolfgin

Stirling Gin

28 October 2015 will always be a special date in the history of Stirling Gin; not only was it the day on which the first ever batch of their premium dry gin was distilled, it also marked the twenty-sixth wedding anniversary of the co-owners, June and Cameron McCann.

Residents of the picturesque Stirlingshire Victorian spa town of Bridge of Allan, the McCann's had launched the first ever Stirling Gin Festival in 2014 to critical acclaim.

Yet despite the success of that maiden foray into the 'botanical world', it was clear that one thing had been missing from the festival… a gin from Stirling!

Subsequently, during long walks with their springer spaniel Kinchie, the McCanns spent hours discussing the possibilities of developing a distinctive gin that was indelibly linked to their historic home city.

It was on one such ramble that June and Cameron realised the vital ingredient needed to create a unique gin that had as its key ingredient an indigenous Stirlingshire herb was staring them, quite literally, in the face.

Growing wild and vital, the Stirlingshire nettle lined the paths of many of the McCanns' strolls through the same historic parkland that had once been hunted by Scotland's medieval rulers, the Stewarts, from their base at the brooding Stirling Castle high above.

The nettle, or correctly speaking *Urtica dioica*, has long been revered and cherished as a life-sustaining herb throughout history, with the ancient Egyptians using nettle infusions for the relief of arthritis and lumbago and the Romans utilising the herb to help stimulate circulation, while the nettle also played a key part in the medical culture of many Native American tribes.

Excited by the prospect of using an essential wild Stirlingshire herb to provide the key ingredient for what would become the first ever Stirling-produced gin, June and Cameron soon set to work.

Painstaking hours of researching and experimenting mounted up as they sought to produce their Holy Grail, a perfect botanical blend that incorporated the Stirlingshire nettle and at the same time provided a scintillating gin that was a wee bit different!

Then, in the spring of 2015, after six torturous months of refining, tasting, distilling and with a little help from a cute copper pot still called Jinty and the tasting buds of a group of loyal and endlessly thirsty friends, the eureka moment finally arrived and the first definitive bottle of Stirling Gin was produced!

Old Smiddy – Stirling Gin.

Boasting a richly intoxicating blend of juniper, basil, angelica, orange, lemon and of course its key ingredient, the wild Stirlingshire nettle, Stirling Gin provides a sensory experience that is like no other on the burgeoning gin scene.

Before long, as demand outstripped supply, Jinty was sadly replaced by a 450-litre copper still called Annie and the production process was refined to provide perfection in a gin glass!

Stirling Gin is cut to 43 per cent ABV. There is no maceration period as Annie is started up straight away, with nettle and basil being placed in the gin basket at the top of the still, while the juniper, angelica, orange and lemon are placed directly in the pot, with each botanical blending process producing a 370-bottle run.

Now just over two years since that eureka moment, Stirling Gin has gathered a string of top accolades and was a finalist in three categories of 2017's inaugural Scottish Gin Society awards, including the blue-ribbon premium dry gin category.

Very shortly Stirling Gin will move home into the customised 'Old Smiddy' distillery, which is situated under the same towering walls of Stirling Castle once trod by the kings and queens of Scotland. #GraspTheNettle!

The Isle of Wight Distillery

Founded in 2015 by Xavier Baker and Conrad Gauntlett, the Isle of Wight Distillery holds the title of the first and only recorded distillery on the island.

They set out to create a premium range of products that reflected the laidback island way of life and true island spirit. With these values at heart each of their handcrafted spirits are a sip of fresh sea air, with crisp, clean and coastal tones invoking memories of a day at the seaside.

The Isle of Wight Distillery started distilling spirits at Rosemary Vineyard, and here it would remain for two years. By the summer of 2017 the ever-growing operation had moved to its permanent home on Pondwell Hill, Ryde. Here their passionate distillers work around the clock to produce our spirits in small batches according to strict recipes using the highest quality fair trade and local ingredients.

Wight Mermaids Gin

Mermaids is a smooth, refreshing gin, capturing the freshness of coastal air from locally foraged rock samphire, citrus notes derived from lemon zest and hints of pepper from the grains of paradise.

This infusion of carefully selected botanicals, including elderflower, coriander seeds and locally grown hops, gives Mermaids a distinct crispness.

Before distilling commences the botanicals are steeped for a whole day and night to allow all of the essential oils to be released. Following this the spirit is distilled for a full day and is left to rest for a further week; never rushed, always adored.

You can enjoy Mermaids with ice cold tonic, ribbons of fresh cucumber and plenty of ice! Inspired by the island's crisp sea air and the hint saltiness on your lips after a day on the open water, it's the ideal tipple to revitalise the body and awaken the senses.

HMS *Victory* Navy Strength Gin

In partnership with the National Museum of the Royal Navy, Victory is a smooth yet commanding Navy Strength Gin with big hits of pepper and oak from grains of paradise and citrus undertones attributed to lemon zest.

Above and Left: Mermaids Gin, Isle of Wight.

Inspired by the Royal Navy's most illustrious warship, HMS *Victory*, our infusion of carefully selected botanicals recreate the style of gin drunk by naval officers during the Battle of Trafalgar.

With a portion of the profits funding the ongoing restoration project of HMS *Victory*, this is our testament to the story of 'Navy Strength' and the heroes who used to enjoy a well-deserved tipple.

Enjoy Victory with ice cold tonic, slices of pink grapefruit and plenty of ice!

Conker Spirit

There is lot of talk about gin these days, with a new gin seeming to pop up on each visit to your favourite watering hole. Short of trying them all, how can you be sure which gin deserves your attention? Conker Spirit has unearthed a little gem from the sunny coast of Dorset that is worth a second look.

Founder and 'Head Conkerer' Rupert Holloway is a fresh face to the drinks industry. Prior to launching Conker Spirit, Dorset's first gin distillery, in April 2015, he worked as a chartered surveyor, a career that took him seven years to train for, and yet had failed to evoke a smile for as long as he dared to remember. The decision to take the leap and work for himself came at the age of twenty-nine, when he had what he calls 'an early midlife crisis', and thought, 'I'll be bitterly disappointed if I retire or die doing what I currently do for a living.' Now almost two years in, Conker Spirit has become a highly regarded mainstay of the gin renaissance, winning multiple awards and national listings including River Cottage, Harvey Nichols and Fortnum & Masons.

Holloway says: 'I thought why are we spoilt for local beers and yet, when it comes to the mighty G&T, our choice is restricted to the industrially distilled brands? So my journey to launch Dorset's first gin distillery began.'

Nestled in the sandy backstreets of Bournemouth, Conker Spirit quietly distil their award-winning Dorset Dry Gin in tiny sixty-bottle batches. And that's just it, Conker Spirit are the real deal; they are the distillers, the bottlers labellers and even the botanical foragers, hand picking New Forest gorse flowers destined for their copper pot still. You see, half the battle with riffling through the flurry of new gins available is knowing which ones are from the genuine, small-batch gin distilleries, doing it for themselves.

Rupert wanted Conker to be a genuine alternative to the mob of London dry gins out there, without being a gimmicky flavoured gin that you politely declined the second time around. So while still remaining a classic dry gin that's true to juniper, the Dorset Dry precisely balances the classic notes of juniper pine and citrus with the fresh, bright and herbaceous notes of elderberries, marsh samphire and hand-picked Dorset gorse flowers.

The Dorset Dry, launched in April 2015, is now the only gin served at River Cottage HQ and has been launched into Fortnum & Mason. Conker Spirit's trophy cabinet is already filling up fast – with awards including a Two Star Great Taste 2015 Award, Gold Taste of the West 2016 Award and a recent gold at the Global Gin Masters 2016.

Conker Gin.

The Conker Gin still.

Conker Gin.

Conker Gin sourcing ingredients.

When poured as a G&T, Conker really comes into its own. To ensure that Conker would stand up proud in a G&T, Holloway incorporated lime peel into Conker's botanical mix, so there is no need for a fancy garnish to make your drink interesting. A Conker and tonic (C&T) is a crisp, refreshing (and extremely quaffable) tipple. Holloway recommends adding just a strip of fresh lime peel to your C&T for the perfect serve.

Conker Spirit work to the mantra 'no gimmicks, no fuss, just top-notch small batch gin distilled in Dorset', and this approach to this subtle twist on a classic gin seems to be working. Mix at your pleasure, but this gin can definitely hold its own.

www.conkerspirit.co.uk

Dyfi Distillery

Dyfi Distillery's journey to establish a small distillery began in 2013, when the founders started discussing a 'dream' to produce gin with a distinct sense of place. That place would be the UNESCO World Biosphere Reserve of the Dyfi Valley. One half of the team,

Pete and Danny at Dyfi Distillery.

Right and below:
Pollination Gin from
Dyfi Distillery.

Pete, had moved here thirty-five years previously to study environmental biology and forgot to leave, and for the last twenty-five years has been foraging, beekeeping and hill farming here. The other half of the team, Danny, had spent all his career working with wine, including as a specialist judge for the Decanter World Wine Awards, and receiving the decoration of Commander of the Order of Prince Henry the Navigator (from the President of Portugal) for services to the wine industry. Danny wanted to transfer that sense of 'terroir' to gin, and, harnessing Pete's foraging knowledge, our journey began.

There are about sixty botanicals we identified in the valley that could be used in gin production, but of that we edited our personal selection down to about half as many, and for Pollination use twenty foraged components, alongside nine classic gin botanicals. Many of the foraged ingredients have ancient connections with alcohol production, such as silver birch sap (for country wine), meadowsweet (for flavouring beer) and bog myrtle (for Gruit Ale).

In 2017, we were honoured to receive the UK Gin of the Year Trophy from the Great British Food Awards. Pollination Gin was first produced in June 2016, and it gained a sibling in March 2017, when we released Hibernation Gin – the world's first gin to be aged in a 100-year-old White Port barrel.

www.dyfidistillery.com

Zufanek, Czech Republic

Zufanek's story began in 2000 when they set up one of the first family run fruit distillery in the Czech Republic. Until then, the majority of fruit brandies were just flavoured vodkas; commercial slivovitz was 90 per cent of vodka and 10 per cent actual plum spirit. Yuck.

As their popularity grew the company decided to focus more on herbal spirits. So in 2008 they introduced our very first distilled absinthe from whole herbs. No artificial colourings, no chemical stuff, simply traditional absinthe as in France in the nineteenth century.

The way Zufanek started the revolution with the first Czech-distilled absinths, they also revolutionised gin.

The idea of creating their own gin popped up at a public tasting event in Brno. After tasting the juniper spirit, people were curious if we planned to make gin. The seed was planted.

There are hundreds of brands of gin on the market, and dozens of excellent ones. So a distiller cannot come up with something worse and then apologise for being a novice in the field. The company's advantage was its six-year experience with making absinthe. It learned a lot about herbs, the maceration period and distillation, and so began to prepare gin in the same way as absinthe, only the herbs were different.

Zufanek made 100 litres and the product simply stunned tasters. They liked it so much that permanent production was decided upon immediately. The only thing that wasn't decided was the name. The very first idea was calling it G-Spot gin. Zufanek even managed to register a trademark as well as the internet domain. A few weeks after making the first batch, they tasted it again and thought, 'Oh, my god, that's so good.' OMG!

OMFG, Zufankek Distillery,
Czech Republic.

OMG, Zufanek Distillery,
Czech Republic.

Zufanek Distillery, Czech Republic.

On 29 December 2013, the first few cases of labelled bottles hit the shelves of the Sklizeno shop in Brno, and the internet-based magazine *Proti šedi* mentioned the gin just a day later.

OMG is currently fourth among the biggest sellers of the Zufanek distillery, and is exported to Germany, Belgium, Switzerland, Italy, Slovakia, Canada, and Singapore.

Forest Gin

Forest Gin is an exceptional, award-winning spirit that is distilled in small batches at a distillery here in the glorious Macclesfield Forest.

Forest Gin is a truly family company. Lindsay and Karl Bond are the husband and wife team in charge of the still, bottling, management, sales and shipping. Harriet Bond (aged eight) is the *boss*. She leads all foraging missions, and is an expert in knowing the best spots for juicy bilberries and ripe raspberries. Hattie would actually prefer it if you did not buy the gin, as any leftover berries end up in her porridge every morning.

Forest Gin aim to make the best tasting gin that they possibly can, from the finest locally sourced ingredients where possible. The company does as much as possible by hand – right down to the bottling.

In 2016, Forest Gin was awarded an unprecedented two separate double gold medals at the San Francisco World Spirit Awards. These awards are the highest accolade within the spirits industry. Therefore, they are proud to say that this places the gin among the world's very finest spirits.

Forest Gin is distilled by the family in batches of a maximum of eighty-five bottles at a time. Each bottle contains these key elements:

Sourced

- Organic juniper berries
- Organic coriander seeds
- Superior quality vanilla pods, liquorice root, angelica and others

Foraged

- Wild bilberries, raspberries and blackberries
- Peak District moss and ferns
- A sprinkling of wild flowers, bark and pin

Water

- The softest forest spring water
- Collected from a spring 1,200 feet above sea level
- An ancient spring in the Peak District
- Blended to 42 per cent ABV

These ingredients are ground by hand using a pestle and mortar, before being distilled in Cheshire. The alcohol vapour and the flavoursome oils from the botanicals reach our copper condenser, where they are immediately cooled. This fragrant spirit is then blended with our spring water to create unfiltered London dry gin of the very highest quality.

The Story of the Amazing Bottle

In a desire to try to source ingredients and materials from within the local area, the natural vessel to hold the gin is Staffordshire Porcelain.

Since 1810, Wade Ceramics have been crafting the highest quality ceramic products, with their items being renowned and collected all over the world. They make bespoke bottles for Forest Gin using many traditional methods, and the final bottle is fully vitrified, meaning they are fired to a temperature that ensures the porcelain will not absorb any moisture, flavour, odour or stains.

The Forest Gin artwork is a one-of-a-kind commission by the respected papercut artist Suzy Taylor. Suzy hand cuts all of her artwork from a single piece of paper using a scalpel and a magnifying glass in a painstaking process.

The team at Wade then apply the artwork by hand to each bottle. The final piece is a practical, yet beautiful, porcelain decanter.

Forest Gin.

The landscape that makes Forest Gin.

Forest Gin and Tonic.

Bottega Bacûr Gin, Italy

This is a distillate produced in Italy based on a recipe of natural ingredients including juniper berries – locally sourced from the surrounding Veneto region at the foot of the Alps – and lemon zest and sage, harvested in the Italian countryside.

The eye-catching bottle is made of blown glass and is glazed with a metallised paint that gives it a warm and refined look that recalls the copper stills (Bacûr means copper in ancient Greek).

This production of this Italian gin benefits from the experience in grappa distillation techniques that Italian distilleries have perfected over the past centuries; indeed, nowadays most of the oenological machinery and alembic stills in the world are made in Italy and designed by Italian engineers.

Focused and expressive on the nose, it opens with an intense and clean scent of juniper, followed by citrus and sage notes, which give a truly Mediterranean flavour. The dry, distinct character lends it to being highly versatile in a range of cocktails, including Bottega's 'Rock and Soul'.

Bottega is a family owned company located in Bibano, Treviso, Italy (45 km north of Venice) that produces and distributes typical Italian premium quality beverages and food products to a global market.

A third-generation business, Bottega is today led by Barbara, Sandro and Stefano Bottega. Headquarters are located in a nineteenth-century farmhouse, renovated to preserve the original architectural and environmental characteristics, surrounded by 10 hectares of vineyards. The group also runs a winery in Valpolicella and one in Montalcino: here, Bottega produces the great red wines of the Veneto and Tuscany, including Amarone and Brunello.

The company manages several different brands, among which are Alexander, Bottega and Cantina dei Poeti. With the goal of producing and distributing the best Italian wine, grappa, spirits, and food all over the world, Bottega advocates quality (Italian taste and authenticity), design (expression of the excellent aesthetic character of being made in Italy) and social responsibility towards the environment and the community.

www.bottegaspa.com

Above and left: Bacur's distinct metallic bottle.

Cotswold Distilling Company

The desire to reflect the natural beauty of the North Cotswolds and honour its heritage runs through everything that is done at the Cotswold Distilling Company. They use local raw materials, traditional kit and techniques, and partner up with other independent producers in the area as much as possible.

They produced a 1616 barrel-aged gin that was created to commemorate the anniversary of Shakespeare's death in 2016. They wanted to have a go at creating the kind of gins that were drunk at the time, which were malt-based genevers rather than neutral spirit-based gins.

www.cotswoldsdistillery.com

Locksley Distilling

Locksley Distilling Company are located in a Grade II listed building in Sheffield. Portland Works is often referred to as the birthplace of stainless steel manufacturing; built in 1879, it is now one of the last remaining working examples of a purpose-built metal trades factory. After many years of neglect the building was brought back to life in 2013 and converted into a thriving social enterprise. The building went through major renovation works to create the historical delight it is today.

Locksley describes themselves as a gin-lover's gin – up front juniper with more delicate aromas of elderflower. It's smooth and round on the palate.

www.locksleydistilling.com

Sipsmith, London

In 2007, two great friends from Cornwall embarked on a mission to bring gin of uncompromising quality and character back to the city where it first earned its name.

After a two-year battle to obtain a distillers license, they triumphantly threw open their little blue doors on Nasmyth Street, Hammersmith, and Sipsmith was born. The launch was to mark the beginning of a gin distilling renaissance in London, and made Sipsmith the first traditional copper pot distillery to open in London for nearly 200 years – something that they're more than just a little bit proud of.

By 2009 Sipsmith had found the perfect location, been granted a license, and commissioned their beautiful copper pot still, Prudence. All that was left was to find a Master Distiller. It was at a Negroni party (of all places) that Sam and Fairfax were introduced to the world-renowned drinks aficionado Jared Brown. It soon became apparent that Jared shared Sam and Fairfax's passion for things well made, and before the evening was out he had agreed to join them on their mission to create the world's best London dry gin.

Sipsmith like to think buildings have a soul. Their original site, on Nasymth Street in Hammersmith, was steeped in alcoholic history; it was once home to the esteemed whisky expert Michael Jackson, and before that was the micro-brewery for a local pub.

Sipsmith founders.

Sipsmith Gin.

Chapter 8

Other Associations and People Passionate About Gin

Today there is much more to gin than just selling and drinking it; a whole world has opened up around the subject. Internationally there are festivals and events such as World Gin Day and Ginfest in Prague, which celebrate the essence of gin and everything that encompasses it and what it has become. Gin has become a part of our culture once again and the brands and businesses of today will become the history of the future.

Mr Fogg's Gin Parlour, London

Around the World in Eighty Days is a classic adventure novel by the French writer Jules Verne, published in 1873. In the story, Phileas Fogg of London and his newly employed French valet Passepartout attempt to circumnavigate the world in eighty days. Mr Fogg's Gin Parlour is modelled on the eccentric explorer's period drawing room, which is laden with artefacts and trinkets collected from his travels. The walls are adorned with everything from stuffed Indian tigers and crocodiles to ornaments collected through his worldwide voyage. Annotated maps and pictures from his travels also feature prominently throughout the bar, as do clocks, given the importance Mr Fogg places on punctuality. A piano for singalongs and an open fireplace to welcome any weary traveller to its hearth also provide focal points. As Fogg was a hero of the Victorian age, guests are able to toast an imposing portrait of its matriarch, Queen Victoria, hanging alongside paintings of him and his ancestors.

Mr Fogg's Residence is a recreation of the Victorian home of Jules Verne's most famous adventurer, Phileas Fogg. Modelled on the very Mayfair house in which Phileas would have lived after travelling around the world in eighty days, the bar is refined, but at the same time truly off the wall, breathing liveliness and fun into the area. Guests are able to encounter all the wonders of the world without setting foot outside of London. As a private man, Mr Fogg's home is of course well-hidden down a small side street off Berkeley Square, thus maintaining an element of secrecy. The project comes from Inception Group, whose founders Charlie Gilkes and Duncan Stirling have also created Chelsea speakeasy Barts, '80s themed nightclub Maggie's, the acclaimed Bunga

Bunga, an Englishman's Italian, bar and pizzeria, karaoke venue Cahoots, a late night 1940s-inspired bar set in a hidden underground tube station and Mr Fogg's Tavern, a Victorian-inspired pub, gin parlour and salon in Covent Garden.

In 2018 the proprietors will throw open the doors at Mr Fogg's Residence, welcoming guests to celebrate the fifth anniversary of the opening of his Mayfair Residence in true Victorian style. Following five years of tremendous expeditions, ground-breaking cocktail menus and welcoming a plethora of renowned explorers into the humble abode, the organisation is celebrating the anniversary with the unveiling of a newly renovated residence and revitalised collection of libations. The magnificent makeover will showcase the completely renovated bar's updated interiors, additional antiques and trinkets that adorn the walls and shelves, as well as additional drawing room arm chairs and seating, all complemented by the innovative sound systems to optimise the venue's acoustics.

Guests are invited the follow the eccentric explorer on his breathtaking adventures through the launch of Mr Fogg's new list of libations in *Phileas' Memoirs, Volume 1: From London to Singapore*. The unique and interactive rotating volvelle menu will feature The £20,000 Wager, highlighting Mr Foggs' first steps at The Reform Club (which includes Hibiscus-infused VII Hills gin, Sipsmith Sloe gin, homemade raspberry leaves syrup, lemon juice, egg white and rhubarb bitter) and First Class Hennessy Hurrah (an aromatic and dry concoction of Hennessy XO cognac, Byrrh Grand

Mr Fogg's Gin Parlour.

Mr Fogg's Residence.

Quinquina aperitif, Martini Riserva Speciale Bitter and Dubonnet aperitif, topped up with Fentimans soda water). The menu, which captures each destination on Phileas' journey, also includes Nocciole Night Train, for those with a lust for cocoa (including hazelnut and cocoa spread-washed Jack Daniel's Gentleman Jack Tennessee whiskey, Calem dry white port, Amaro Lucano bitters and maple syrup). A Southerly African Scent takes its inspiration from Phileas' trail through the Isthmus of Suez (served using Bacardi Oro rum, Alipus San Juan mezcal, homemade African spice falernum, Pimento bitters, sugar syrup and fresh lime juice). A stop off at Singapore marks a symbolic halfway point within the journey around the world; indulge in the herbaceous and rich concoction of Jungle Flora (served with chamomile-infused Russian Standard vodka, ginger liqueur, Green Chartreuse liqueur, lime juice, egg white, homemade sugar syrup and citrus foam).

A quote from Charlie Gilkes, one of the founders:

Mr Fogg's is a quirky Victorian-inspired bar concept for the adventurous. Based on the fictional explorer Phileas Fogg and his infamous travels, the brand takes inspiration from all over the globe, illustrated in both its menus and interiors. First to open was his eccentric residence located in a back street in Mayfair, stuffed with artefacts and antiquities collected on his many adventures. The eclectic gin parlour and tavern followed, located in Covent Garden and opening after the sad passing of Fogg's late Aunt Gertrude by her former servant Fanny McGee.

Emporia Brands, Surrey

Emporia Brands is a spirits importer, exporter and innovator that is relentless in seeking, from around the world, distillers who respect artisan traditions of quality, in both the ingredients and process, and shun industrial shortcuts in the pursuit of truly great drinks. They have made many friends among these producers – in some cases now over three generations – and these brands all have great reputations as a result of their craft methods of production. The small talented Emporia team now reach every market for fine spirits, including independent merchants and retailers, and, thanks to a network of highly skilled distributors, to bars at every level nationally, including the nation's world-class bartenders. Their record of innovation is in bringing most of their brands to the UK market for the first time and, in collaboration with bartenders and retail partners, developing exciting new spirit libations.

Hoxton Gin

For the past twenty-five years Hoxton has been the creative centre of London; a heady mixture of artists, writers and rock stars mixing seamlessly with super models, fashion designers and entrepreneurs cross-pollinating ideas and changing the way everyone else does things.

This is where street artist Banksy went from doorways and alleys to the auction house, where there's always a buzz in the air which feels as if anything can happen. And you know what? Knowing Hoxton, it probably will.

Hoxton Gin was created by East End drinks maverick Gerry Calabrese, who has built a reputation as one of the greats in London's bar and club scene. From bartending in top London venues such as Lab, Dust and Sex in the City, he went on to launch his own multi-award winning East End bar, The Hoxton Pony, followed most recently in 2016 by Wringer + Mangle, situated in the neighbouring London Fields, to much critical acclaim. His pedigree has also seen him act as drinks columnist for *Arena* magazine as well as consultant and event planned for numerous high-profile private clients included Giles Deacon, Swarvoski, Peroni Nasto Azzuro, Channel 4, Mulberry, New Look and Dinh Van. Hoxton Gin is currently produced at one of the world's leading micro-distillers and is created using the finest ethically sources ingredients.

Quality is key so they've only used a medley of natural and ethically sources ingredients, including juniper, iris, tarragon and ginger, which are macerated for five days before single distillation in a 150-year-old copper pot still to obtain the perfect and ultra-smooth distillate, which is blended with their premium grain spirit and then finished with natural coconut and pink grapefruit. Hoxton Gin is then filtered and rested in steel tanks for two months while all the natural botanicals harmonise.

Mayfield Sussex Hop Gin

'A diabolically delectable gin from the home of the good Saint Dunstan, Mayfield'.

The story of Mayfield Sussex Hop Gin starts on a single farm in East Sussex, where columns of hops rise to the sky. They harvest those hops, dry them in their oast house, and distil them in a copper pot still. The twist? They then infuse and distil it with seven natural botanicals (juniper, orange peel, lemon peel, coriander seeds, angelica, orris and liquorice).

Sussex Hop – Their variety of hop was found growing local in Sussex hedgerows before it was cultivated by award-winning sixth-generation hop farmer Andrew Hoad. This variety of hop brings a very unique floral note and some bitter-sweetness supported by the fresh, zesty citrusy notes.

Juniper – Juniper berries are the primary botanical in gin. The juniper gives Mayfield Gin a traditional character as well as some body, along with green, pine, woody and spicy notes.

Orange Peel – Orange peel and segments are often used as botanicals in gin, both fresh and dry, due to the distinctive citrus notes. Mayfield Gin uses dry orange peel as a botanical to add freshness to their blend.

Lemon Peel – Lemon peel is another common citrus fruit used in gin. Working with the orange peel, Mayfield Gin uses lemon peel to add further complexity to the citrus notes but also to add a very slight bitterness.

Coriander Seeds – Coriander seeds are used in Mayfield Gin to enhance the fresh and zesty notes from the Sussex Hop. Coriander seeds are hugely important in gin production and are actually the second most commonly used botanical after juniper.

Angelica – Angelica root is a common botanical used throughout the history of gin. The root is normally used but distillers have been known to use seeds and sometimes even the flower. Mayfield Gin uses angelica root to bring subtle earthy notes with a dry taste.

Orris – The iris flower is common throughout the world and its roots have been used as a botanical in gin for quite some time. Orris roots takes years to grow to a point of harvest, when they are then picked and ground to a fine powder. Known for their unique floral, sweet smell, they are used to fix the aromas and bind the other botanicals.

Liquorice – The sweet and woody botanical has been used as a sugar alternative for centuries. However, don't confuse this with liquorice sweets ... this botanical brings out a unique woody taste and works extremely well with angelica root, creating that distinctive dry, earthy taste.

Mayfield Sussex Hop Gin was created by James Rackham, founder of artisanal spirits company Emporia Brands, liveryman of The Worshipful Company of Distillers and resident of Mayfield Village, East Sussex. The dramatic label depicts the story of Saint Dunstan and the Devil, an epic event that, as the story goes, happened in the tenth century in Mayfield Village. There is an old saying, which can be found on the bottle: 'Saint Dunstan, as the story goes, once pull'd the devil by the nose ... with red hot tongs which made him roar ... that he was heard, three miles or more!'

Emporia Brands Mayfield, Sussex Hop Gin.

The hops used in Mayfield Gin were discovered as a wild hop growing in local hedgerows around the Mayfield, East Sussex area. This variety of hop is now cultivated in just 1 acre of a 30-acre hop farm in Salehurst. Sussex Hop is now an approved variety and gives an amazing citrus and hop character to the fabulous Mayfield Gin.

Jindea Single Estate Tea Gin

'A citrus-forward gin with aromatic spices, peaches and apricots.'

'J' represents the juniper botanical; 'INDE' is French for India (made in a French distillery); 'EA' represents tea. Preferred pronunciation – JIN-DEE-AH.

The brand is a result of a partnership between three bar scene experts, including Matthew Dakers and Jack Rackham of Emporia, a London-based spirit distribution and export company and Adrian Gomes, owner of two Scottish bars and events company 10 Dollar Shake.

Emporia Brands, Jindea Gin.

Emporia Brands, Jindea.

The spirit is produced in a traditional alembic copper pot still to a classic London dry gin recipe containing ten botanicals, including Darjeeling tea.

As well as the subtle flavours from Darjeeling tea, the gin contains flavours of juniper, lemon, grapefruit, coriander, ginger, fennel, cardamom, cinnamon and angelica. They are confident that the spirit the collective has created will have both local and international appeal.

The team enlisted a tea comelier, Ajit Madan, co-founder of Camellia's Tea House in London and the UK's first certified International Tea Education Institute (ITEI) Master Tea Sommelier. Ajit introduced the makers to a first flush Darjeeling tea from the Goomtee Estate, a single estate tea plantation in the Kurseong Valley, India.

Darjeeling tea imparts aromas of muscatel grape and stone fruits. It is known as the 'Champagne of Teas' and the picturesque artisan tea gardens of Darjeeling, at the foot of the Himalayas, produce less than 1 per cent of India's total tea production. This is mostly from single estates and is often organic and hand plucked.

Darjeeling is a black tea that produces four harvest throughout the year, known as 'flushes'. The first flush is the spring picking, which produces the gentlest of black teas. This and the second flush are the most desirable and it's the first flush Jindea have selected to impart gentle qualities to their gin.

Darjeeling Goomtee Exotic Thunder First Flush is a single origin tea, grown in the world-famous Goomtee Tea Garden in the stunning Kurseong Valley. It is grown organically and in high altitudes, ensuring its highest quality and exceptional character. As with any delicate first flush tea, Exotic Thunder has a very short harvest time and is carefully plucked for just two weeks in March.

Its long leaves show a delightful range of colours, from delicate emerald to bold olive, with a gentle scattering of fuzzy silver buds. Once brewed, Exotic Thunder produces a vibrant and glossy infusion, reminiscent of pale honey with an unmistakable aroma of apricots and floral notes. The cup is unbelievably smooth and crisp, with hints of grapes and sweet young vegetables, augmented by floral overtones. Its beautifully balanced astringency is a clear mark of a well-made first flush Darjeeling tea.

The Goomtee tea estate itself was first established in 1899 by a British tea planter, Henry Lennox, and at one point it was even owned by the royal family of the Ranas in Nepal. The estate is well known for its remarkable black teas, as well as the beautiful vistas of the valley and surrounding mountains, making it a popular travel destination for many tea connoisseurs.

Saffron Gin

Emporia Brands, Saffron Gin.

'Intense and exotic … a rediscovered recipe.'

Knowledge and expertise of more than 140 years is at the heart of Gabriel Boudier, a name that is renowned worldwide. Since its foundation in 1874, Gabriel Boudier has invented and diversified into a range of exceptional products that delight enthusiasts. Gabriel Boudier is now synonymous with authentic tastes, which they invite you to discover, enjoy and share with them.

Saffron Gin comes from a recipe rediscovered in the Boudier archives. Saffron Gin is the result of an alliance between Great Britain for its London dry gin, India for its spice, used extensively in cooking and in religious ceremonies, and French know-how. This original product with exotic notes is manufactured entirely at Dijon and is used in numerous cocktails, the most famous being gin and tonic.

The richness or the colour and the aroma delight the senses, offering an enchanting combination of juniper, citrus and angelica – an exotic delight.

Emporia Brands Mayfield, Sussex Hop Gin.

Gin Foundry

Gin Foundry calls itself the home of gin. It is a hub for those who seek out more information about the spirits they're drinking; not just how they taste, but how they're made and by whom. As well as reviews, it shares news, insight, interviews and cocktail recipes to keep readers up to date as the category evolves. Everything they do is underpinned by a singular driving ethos: to celebrate gin.

Gin Foundry now has a raft of projects to its name: the Ginvent Calendar, Junipalooza, the Ginfographic and the Ginsmith Awards, as well as a sister shop – Gin Kiosk. The organisation also provides workshops and master classes for those interested in opening their own distilleries. Gin Foundry is a resource for gin fans and makers alike.

Who are the Gin Foundry team?

Olivier Ward

As editor and co-founder of Gin Foundry, Olivier oversees the content on the website as well as the creative direction of its projects. With years of experience building drinks brands, distilling gin and writing about it, he is well placed to comment on the category and does his best to cast a positive light on the spirit and those making it.

Olivier also delivers consultancy work for those seeking to open their own distilleries and hosts frequent 'How to open a distillery' workshops at Gin Foundry HQ. He is shortlisted as IWSC's Communicator of the Year 2017 and has been named by *USA Today* as one of the foremost specialist authorities on gin. Outside of his work on Gin Foundry's platforms, Olivier is Channel 4's resident gin expert on *Sunday Brunch,* has presented sections on gin cocktails for ITV *This Morning* and features regularly talking about the category on BBC radio. He has also contributed articles about gin to *Olive Magazine, BA Highlife, N by Norwegian, The Gentlemen's Journal* and *Ask Men.*

Emile Ward

Emile is the engineer behind Gin Foundry, responsible for keeping the wheels turning. He handles social media, manages bespoke projects and organises events from start to finish. His commercial understanding has allowed Gin Foundry to launch products that promote the category, allowing consumers to enjoy all aspects of gin's rich history, and has also led to the success of Gin Kiosk.

Emile has grown Gin Kiosk to such an extent that it is now stepping into its own shoes, with a clearer demarcation from Gin Foundry in order to keep the editorial and commercial transparency clear. Expect to see Emile and Gin Kiosk host pop-ups and events in partnerships with the best ginsmiths the world over. Under Emile's careful stewardship, the Ginvent calendars have gone global, while Junipalooza is not only the most respected gin event in the UK has seen, but in Australia, too.

Leah Gasson

When Leah joined the team, she had a thirst for gin that far surpassed her knowledge on the subject matter. She has spent years fully immersed in a cloud of juniper, learning all that she can about gin as she revelled in its history and soaked up the stories from each and every maker out there.

As staff writer, Leah is responsible for generating the editorial content on Gin Foundry, from reviews, to news, to cocktail recipes and interviews. She also writes both Gin Foundry and Gin Kiosk's newsletters, as well as their yearly hardback book – the *Gin Annual*.

Olivier and Emile of the Gin Foundry.

Olivier of the Gin Foundry.

The Gin Foundry.

Gin Monkey

Who is the Gin Monkey?

The Gin Monkey is one woman (Emma) on a mission to make the world of cocktail drinking more accessible to the masses. London based, she works in science in the daytime and as a bartender in cocktail bars on occasional evenings, hosting gin tastings and generally hanging out in gin distilleries whenever possible. She has published her first book, *The Periodic Table of Cocktails.*

She also runs World Gin Day, which takes place on the second Saturday of June every year, and has worked as a gin tutor and bartender across multiple cities.

Why the Gin Monkey Site was Born

When Emma moved to London she struggled to find good cocktail bars, so in November 2009 ginmonkey.co.uk was born with an aim to create a site that focused on cocktail bars specifically, and was built on the ideals of being independent and impartial.

However, as time went on it became impossible to keep up this anonymity, plus more and more exciting opportunities were being presented to Emma that wouldn't work if she was anonymous. Plus, there were finally new sites emerging that were reviewing cocktail bars on their merits and had teams behind them that could cover London more

The Gin Monkey.

effectively than she ever could (like Design My Night). All of this combined meant it was time to put the reviewing to bed and focus on spirits, cocktails and specifically (though not exclusively) Gin Evolution... and the story behind the name

Emma's journey has taken a lot of twists and turns along the way. She named the site Gin Monkey because of her love of the juniper spirit and the fact that she has got ridiculously long arms (!) rather than with an intention to write about gin specifically. However, over the years she has been invited to, and been given access to, so much information about gin that she's ended up being swept along with the amazing revival the spirit has recently undergone.

Consequently, the site is now where Emma indulges her love of gin, cocktails and more. You won't find formal reviews, as she simply doesn't have time to do this comprehensively (there are other sites with teams behind them that do this – check out Gin Foundry for one!). Instead, Emma try to use the insight that she has into the gin and cocktail world to put together interesting articles and content that approaches things a little differently!

World Gin Day

The concept is simple: get people enjoying gin together all over the world. It is a day for everyone and anyone (over drinking age of course...!) to celebrate and enjoy gin! Whether you're already a fan of the juniper spirit, or looking for an intro, World Gin Day is the perfect opportunity to get involved.

So When Does World Gin Day Take Place?

World Gin Day is always the second Saturday in June. This means the date moves around a little year on year but does allow Sunday to recover!

Who's Behind World Gin Day?

Founded by Neil Houston in 2009, it started off as a day to bring his friends together to drink gin! It has been run by Emma Stokes, aka Gin Monkey, since 2013, and has evolved into a truly global celebration with events running in over thirty countries around the world, reaching over 50 million people on social channels.

Ginfest, Prague, Czech Republic

Ginfest by Barlife is an educational and entertainment event for the public as well as a professional audience. The event involves the tasting of dozens of brands of specific spirits. Thematic catering, decorations and music are always included. At these event, visitors have the opportunity to taste a great variety of quality spirits and attend seminars, guided tastings and workshops, while professionals can participate in bartenders' competitions.

Gin selection in shop window. (Image courtesy of Jason Neale)

Bibliography

Arnold, Catherine, *Necropolis London and its Dead* (London: Pocket Books, 2008).

Colquhoun, Kate, *Taste – The Story of Britain through its Cooking* (London: Bloomsbury, 2007).

Flanders, Judith, *The Victorian City* (London: Atlantic Books, 2012).

Funnel, Barry, *The America Ground* (unknown details).

Ginn, Peter and Ruth Goodman, *Wartime Farm* (London: Mitchell Beazley, 2012).

Picard, Liza, *Victorian London The Life of a City 1840–1870* (London: Phoenix, 2006).

Stevens Curl, James, *Victorian Architecture* (London: Spire 1990).

www.gin-bottles.com, accessed January 2018.

www.insider-london.co.uk, February 2018.

About the Author

Tina Brown was born and brought up in Hastings, East Sussex, and has always had a passion for history. Tina has her own tour guide business, which was started in 1992 and prides itself on providing bespoke and high-quality guided tours and street theatre, which Tina researches, writes and produces herself. She likes to bring history to life in new and memorable ways.

Acknowledgements

The author and publisher would like to thank the following people/organisations for permission to use copyright material in this book: York Museums Trust (http://yorkmuseumstrust.org.uk/); the British Museum; and the British Newspaper Archives.

Every attempt has been made to seek permission for copyright material used in this book. However, if we have inadvertently used copyright material without permission/acknowledgement, we apologise and we will make the necessary correction at the first opportunity.

Image Acknowledgements

I would like to thank the generosity of everyone that supplied images to use in this book. Many thanks to York Museums Trust and the British Museum for their support in providing some of the historical image content. Thanks also to Bill Brown (gin-bottles.com) for kindly helping and supplying historical images throughout the book; to Jason Neale (jason@blackorangepress.com); and to M. L. Bernabeu and J. Garland (Underground Overground Archaeology).